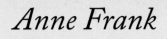

Anne Frank

Anne Frank

by Rachel Epstein

A FIRST BOOK

Franklin Watts
A Division of Grolier Publishing
New York - London - Hong Kong - Sydney
Danbury, Connecticut

Cover and interior design by Molly Heron
Cover illustration by Nechama Goldfinger
Frontis illustration by Shira Pfeffer
Special thanks to Professor Marjorie Trenk, Stern College for Women, Yeshiva University

Photographs ©: Archive Photos: 33, 34 top, 44 (James McAnally), 18 (Potter Collections),
12, 14, 25, 34, 56 (Sony Pictures/fotos international), 6, 22, 48;
Gamma-Liaison: 55 (Guerrini-Liaison); Novosti/Corbis-Bettmann: 50;
Reuters/Corbis-Bettmann: 53; Rijksinstituut voor Oorlogsdocumentatie,
Netherlands State Institute for War Documentation: 30, 46;
UPI/Corbis-Bettmann: 8, 17, 20, 27, 28, 36, 42, 51, 54.

All quotations of the diary of Anne Frank from
The Diary of a Young Girl: The Definitive Edition
by Anne Frank.
Otto H. Frank & Mirjam Pressler, Editors,
translated by Susan Massotty.
Translation copyright © 1995 by Doubleday,
a division of Bantam Doubleday Dell Publishing Group, Inc.
Used by permission of Doubleday, a division of
Bantam Doubleday Dell Publishing Group, Inc.

Library of Congress Cataloging-in-Publication Data

Epstein, Rachel
Anne Frank / by Rachel Epstein

p.   cm.—(A First book)
Includes bibliographical references and index.
Summary: Traces the life of a Jewish girl who chronicled her
day-to-day life in a diary as she hid
in an attic in Nazi-occupied Holland for two years.
ISBN O-531-20298-4 (lib. bdg.)   0-531-15883-7 (pbk.)
1. Frank, Anne, 1929–1945—Juvenile literature.   2. Jewish children in the Holocaust—Netherlands—Amsterdam—Biography—Juvenile literature.   3. Amsterdam (Netherlands)—Biography—
Juvenile literature.   [1. Frank, Anne, 1929–1945.   2. Jews—Netherlands—Biography.   3. Holocaust, Jewish (1939–1945)—Netherlands—Amsterdam.   4. Women—Biography.]   I. Title.
II. Series.
DS135.N6F334   1997
940.563'18'092—dc21
[b]   96–51192   CIP   AC

Contents

Introduction

ANNE FRANK WAS a Jewish girl born in Frankfurt, Germany, in 1929. If she had not been Jewish, or if she had been born in a different time or place, she might have grown up to be a famous journalist or even a movie star, as she had dreamed. Today, she might have a husband, children, and grandchildren. But she lived when Adolf Hitler came to power in Germany, so she was forced to go into hiding for two years. She kept a diary, filled with descriptions of her daily life and her hopes and fears. Unfortunately, Hitler's work killed Anne.

Adolf Hitler wanted to kill all the Jews in Europe. Working through the Nazi Party, he killed six million of them—two out of every three Jews in Europe at the time. This mass killing of Jews, called the Holocaust, happened during World War II. One of the reasons Hitler was able to carry out the Holocaust was that Germany had defeated almost all the countries in Europe.

In the Holocaust, Jews were rounded up and sent by train to labor camps, called concentration camps. Six of these camps were death camps, built specifically for the killing of the Jews. Special Nazi police called the Gestapo ran the camps. The Gestapo had many ways of killing Jews, but the most common was poison gas. When a trainload of Jews arrived at a camp, those who were too weak, too sick, too young, or too old to work were gassed immediately. The others were kept as slave laborers to make equipment that Germany needed to fight the war. Most died of starvation, disease, or exposure to the cold.

Hitler thought that Germans were superior people and that they had to remain pure, which meant never marrying anyone inferior. He considered Jews, gypsies, homosexuals, and people with disabilities inferior, but his feelings were particularly strong against the Jews. He wrote these ideas in a book called *Mein Kampf*, which means "my struggle," published in 1924.

Hundreds of thousands of people helped Hitler carry out the "Final Solution," which is what the Nazis called their plan for the extermination of the Jews. Millions of

Hitler, May 1934, giving a speech for radio

others saw what was happening and made no attempt to stop it. There were, however, as Anne Frank's story shows, some good and brave people who tried to keep Jews safe.

Prejudice against Jews had existed for hundreds of years before Hitler came to power in 1933. Jews were restricted in their work, land ownership, rank in the army, and places they could live. Sometimes they were actually forced out of a country. And sometimes they were murdered. But the Holocaust was the first time that a government had as its goal the total, systematic destruction of all the members of a particular group just because they belonged to that group.

Eventually, in 1945, after six years of war, Hitler's enemies defeated him. But by then, Anne Frank had been killed in the Holocaust. Hiding could not save her. She was fifteen years old when she died.

Europe 1943-1944

Anne called this 1930 picture of her and Margot with their father "Papa with his kids" when she put it in a photo album several years after it was taken. Anne and Margot adored their father.

ONE

Facing Prejudice

ANNE FRANK'S FATHER, Otto Frank, was a businessman in Frankfurt, Germany, where his family had lived for many generations. He had been in the German army during World War I, which ended with Germany's defeat by England, France, the United States, and other countries. This defeat left many Germans feeling disgraced. They thought a military victory would restore their honor.

When Hitler's Nazi Party was voted into power in elections in Frankfurt in 1933, Otto Frank decided to move his family out of Germany. He accepted an offer to run a company in the Netherlands called Opekta-Works. Opekta made pectin, a substance that makes fruit juice harden into jelly. The Netherlands (which is also called Holland, and whose people are called Dutch) was an appealing new home because it had a tradition of acceptance of all different types of people, including Jews. It is also

next to Germany, so the Franks would not be moving far away.

Anne Frank was four years old when her family moved to Amsterdam, Holland's largest city. Mr. Frank had gone on ahead to find a new house. She moved with her mother, Edith Frank-Holländer, her sister, Margot, who was then seven, and her grandmother, who died before the family went into hiding. Anne attended a Montessori school in Amsterdam, where she liked everything except math. She was a good student but had a tendency to talk a lot to her friends in class, which bothered some of her teachers.

As a little girl, Anne loved fun and getting into mischief. She enjoyed going to the movies and the beach, reading and writing, playing Ping-Pong, and riding her bicycle. Her friend Hanne Goslar, who had also moved to Amsterdam from Germany, recalled Sunday trips to the Opekta factory, where the two girls would amuse themselves by calling each other from room to room on the

Anne at school; she was a good student but did not like math and had a tendency to talk so much in class that her teachers became annoyed.

telephones. They also used to stand on the Franks' apartment balcony and pour water on the people below.

The Goslars were traditional Jews, meaning they paid attention to all the Jewish religious holidays, while the Franks were Reform Jews—they celebrated only some Jewish holidays and tended to live more like their Christian neighbors. On Friday evenings, the beginning of the Jewish Sabbath, the Frank family would often visit the Goslars. Although Anne's mother and sister occasionally went to the synagogue (Jewish house of worship), Anne and her father had little interest in religious activities.

Miep Gies, a Dutch Christian woman who worked at Opekta, and her husband, Jan, often had Sunday dinner at the Frank house. Miep played an important part in helping the Frank family in hiding, and she also discovered Anne's diary after the Frank family had been rounded up by the Nazis. Miep remembers Anne as an outspoken girl who was interested in the world around her. She also recalled that Anne spent a lot of time brushing and setting her thick, dark brown hair.

Anne Frank described her own life when she was twelve years old as "heavenly" and said it was filled with friends and male admirers. She also said she was "spoiled rotten" by her parents and got a lot of candy and a large allowance. She saw herself as cleverly witty, flirty, and amusing, which helped to make her the center of attention in school and at parties. But Anne also had a more

🝑 *120,000 followers of Hitler assemble at a rally in Nuremberg, Germany, to hear him speak. Hitler spoke of the Jews as inferior people who were responsible for all the problems in Germany.*

serious side that she described as "hardworking, honest and generous . . . and I wasn't stuck up."

While Anne was enjoying a normal life in Holland, Hitler and the Nazis were making life more and more

Flames engulfed synagogues in Germany and Austria on Kristallnacht, November 9, 1938. Nazi sympathizers destroyed property and murdered one hundred Jews.

difficult for the Jews who still lived in Germany. Jewish schoolchildren were shouted at, spat on, and bullied by their German classmates. Massive rallies took place in which Jews were described as evil monsters. These incidents had caused some Jews, like the Franks, to leave the country. But others thought they could stay in Germany and wait for things to get better.

The events of *Kristallnacht*, though, made German Jews realize that things were going to get worse instead of better. On November 9, 1938, roving bands of Nazis and other Germans, encouraged by the government, attacked all the synagogues and many of the Jewish businesses and homes in Germany. They broke windows (*Kristallnacht* means "night of broken glass" in German) and wrote anti-Jewish slogans on the walls. They also killed one hundred Jews and beat up many more. They rounded up thirty thousand Jewish men and sent them to labor camps far from their families.

On May 10, 1940, a year and a half after *Kristallnacht,* the Germans attacked Holland. Only four days later, the Dutch surrendered and the Nazis took over the government. By 1941, the Nazis in Holland began restricting the activities of the Jews.

Step by step, the freedoms and privileges Jews had enjoyed were taken away from them. They were not allowed to stay in hotels or go to movies, restaurants, libraries, or public parks. They had to turn in their radios. They had to register with the German authorities, and a large black "J" was stamped on the identity cards that all Dutch people had to carry with them. This meant the Germans knew who the Jews were and where they lived, which was important information when they began rounding up Jews. Any Jews who failed to register were to be put in prison for five years.

Jews could not marry non-Jews, they could not visit Christians, and they could not sit outside in their own gardens or their friends' gardens after 8:00 in the evening. They could not be on the street between 8:00 at night and 6:00 the next morning. They could not ride in cars—even their own cars. They could not use streetcars. They

The writing on an eyeglass store window in Vienna says "Jude," the German word for Jew, and displays a swastika, the twisted cross that was the symbol of the Nazi Party. It warned Viennese Christians, after the Nazi invasion of Austria in March 1938, not to patronize this store because its owner was Jewish.

had to put their bicycles into perfect working order and then turn them over to the German authorities. These restrictions meant that the only way the Jews could move around was by walking.

Jews had to do all their shopping between 3:00 and 5:00 in the afternoon, and they could only go to certain stores. They could only use barbershops and beauty parlors owned by Jews. They could not use swimming pools, tennis courts, hockey fields, or rowboats, and they could not take part in team sports. They had to wear a big yellow star with the word "Jude," which means "Jew," sewn into it.

Jews were prohibited from working for the government or for businesses owned by Dutch Christians. Also, they could no longer own their own businesses and had to turn them over to non-Jews (which is what happened to Opekta). This meant they were unemployed. The Germans sent unemployed men to labor camps. There they worked the Jews so hard and gave them so little food and clothing, even in bitterly cold weather, that most of the prisoners died within a few months.

Jewish children could not attend schools that were not specifically Jewish. Anne Frank left the Montessori school and went to the Jewish Lyceum, where her sister Margot was already a student.

The effect of these laws was to isolate the Jews from everyone else in Holland, which meant it was almost impossible to be close to Dutch Christians who might be willing and able to help them avoid the persecutions of the Nazis. Not being able to work also meant they became poorer and poorer.

In her first diary entries in the summer of 1942, Anne wrote casually about being excluded from ice cream parlors and streetcars. She seemed more concerned about boys and grades and teachers than about these restrictions. But she also knew her situation as a Jew was extremely dangerous. She wrote that "nothing else mattered" except getting safely into hiding.

The front of the offices of Opekta-Works, number 263 Prinsengracht in Amsterdam

TWO

In Hiding

OTTO FRANK KNEW that the Nazi occupation of Holland meant his family was in danger. In the spring and summer of 1941, Nazis were already killing Jews in Poland, which they had defeated in September 1939, and Russia, which they were fighting to defeat. Mr. Frank began making plans for his family to hide in a secret annex behind the attic of his office building. He hoped they would be safe there until the Germans could be driven out of Holland. Going into hiding was illegal, but Otto Frank thought it was worth the risk.

He planned to take the family into hiding in the middle of July 1942, but on June 29, Dutch newspapers said that all Jews were going to be rounded up and sent to concentration camps. On the morning of July 5, Mr. Frank told Anne he had been bringing furniture and clothing to a place he considered safe. That afternoon, Margot, who was sixteen, received a card ordering her to report the next day. No one knew where she would be sent. Otto Frank decided that instead of letting Margot report, the family would go into hiding immediately.

Anne packed her diary, hair curlers, a comb, schoolbooks, and old letters. When she explained in her diary why she had chosen these things and not others, she said, "Memories mean more to me than dresses."

The next morning, it was raining so hard that the police were not out patrolling the street. This was lucky for the Franks. Because they could not use any transportation or suitcases, moving was extremely difficult. Anne wrote that she had to walk across Amsterdam and into hiding wearing "two undershirts, three pairs of underpants, a dress, and over that a skirt, a jacket, a raincoat, two pairs of stockings, heavy shoes, a cap, a scarf and lots more." The Franks left their home in a mess, partly because they did not have time to clean up, but also because they wanted to leave the impression that they had fled to Switzerland, where Otto Frank's mother lived. This way, no one would look for them in Amsterdam.

We know about Anne's life in hiding from what she wrote in her diary. Her parents had given it to her for her thirteenth birthday, June 12, 1942—just a few weeks before the family went into hiding. Anne called the diary "Kitty."

In her first entry, she wrote that she hoped to tell it things that were more important than the everyday

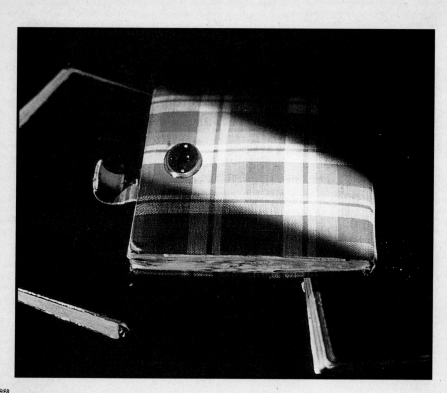

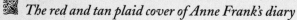 *The red and tan plaid cover of Anne Frank's diary*

things she talked about with her friends. She hoped the diary would be "a great source of comfort and support." She stored it in her father's old leather briefcase and never wrote in it when other people were around, even in the close quarters of her hiding place.

A week after the Franks went into hiding, they were joined by the Van Pels family (called the Van Daans in the diary): Hermann Van Pels, Otto Frank's business partner, his wife, Auguste, their sixteen-year-old son, Peter, and a cat. A little later, the Franks' dentist, Fritz Pfeffer (called Albert Dussel in the diary) joined them. Dr. Pfeffer brought news that Jews in Amsterdam were being rounded up and sent to crowded camps where there was hardly any food or water.

Anne had some idea of what was happening from peeking out the window. She saw the police ordering people about in the streets and beating them. She wrote, "No one is spared. The sick, the elderly, children, babies, and pregnant women—all are marched to their death. . . . And all because they're Jews."

Life in hiding meant never going outside. Anne was luckier than most of the thousands of Jews in hiding throughout Europe because when Opekta's workers went home she could leave the annex and go into the factory. But she missed the sky, the sun, school, and normal life. "All I really want," she wrote, "is to be an honest-to-goodness teenager." Being in hiding meant being quiet most of the day. It also meant living in terror of being discovered.

Anne did many things to try to make her life as normal as possible. She studied a lot because she enjoyed it and because she did not want to be behind when she went back to school after the war. She studied history, which she loved, math, which she called "awful" and

German and Dutch police stopping civilians in Holland and demanding to
see their identity papers

"wretched," and English, French, geography, the Bible,
and Greek and Roman mythology.

She and her sister, Margot, helped Opekta by filing
papers and making out bills at night. They also practiced
shorthand, which secretaries use to take notes quickly.
Anne loved to read Dutch books and plays. She engaged
in what she called a "dance and ballet craze," using her

🔳 *This aerial view of Amsterdam shows the office and annex. The courtyard in the center of the picture contained a chestnut tree that provided natural cover for the annex windows, except in winter, when the leaves were gone. Anne loved to look up at the Westertoren Church steeple, on the right.*

mother's slip as a costume. She did exercises so she would be as limber as she had been before going into hiding. She also helped with kitchen chores.

Anne spent a lot of time writing. She loved writing in her diary and writing stories. Her stories were often about girls who were unsure of themselves and who were misunderstood by their mother. Underneath Anne's confident exterior, this is how she saw herself.

In March 1944, after the family had been in hiding for more than one and a half years, Anne heard on the radio that when the war was over the government would collect the writings of people in hiding. She began revising her diary entries and copying them out, hoping her writing would be seen by others.

Living in hiding required non-Jewish helpers. The helpers for the annex were Miep Gies and Bep Voskuijl, secretaries at Opekta, and Johannes Kleiman and Victor Kugler, the men to whom Mr. Frank had turned over ownership of the business. Miep's husband and Bep's father also helped.

The helpers shopped for food and other necessities. They used the money of the people in hiding and ration cards made by members of the Dutch Underground, who were resisting the Nazis in Holland. Ration cards entitled their owners to purchase stated amounts of items that were in short supply, such as cooking oil and sugar. The helpers also brought new library books and returned the old ones every week.

They had to work without arousing the suspicion of anyone else in the business or of people in the street, who might have wondered why bags of food were being brought into an office. Their enemies were not only the German occupiers but also members of the Dutch Nazi Party. People received rewards for turning in those in hiding and their helpers.

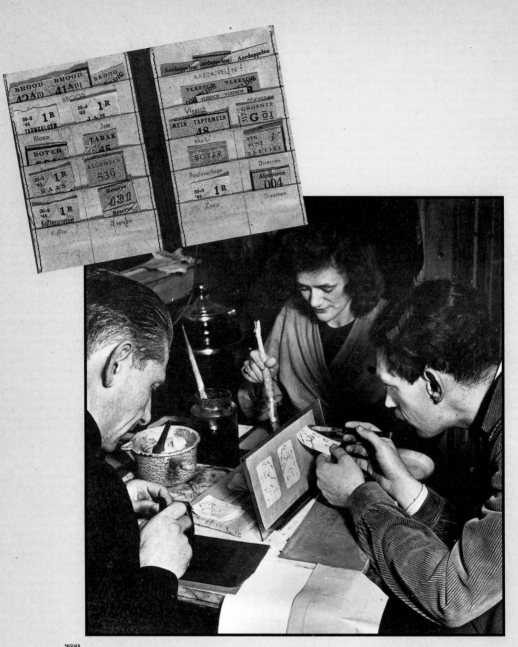

(top) Dutch rationing coupons; (bottom) members of the Dutch Underground forging identity cards, which helped Jews avoid capture

The helpers were a valuable link to the outside world, and their visits made living in hiding a little less boring. Every day when the rest of the Opekta workers went home for lunch, the helpers came upstairs. They brought in the needed supplies and stayed for coffee after lunch. Then everyone listened to the radio together for news of the war. The helpers also went up after the last workers had gone home for the day to let their friends know it was safe to move around and talk above a whisper.

Anne's mood was always changing. She went from being sad to happy to sad again. In hiding, without the many distractions of the outside world, it was easy for Anne to focus attention on her own feelings. Once, when she was feeling sad, she wrote, "I simply can't imagine the world will ever be normal again for us. I do talk about 'after the war,' but it's as if I were talking about a castle in the air, something that can never come true."

Later, on a day of clear weather, she wrote, "The best remedy for those who are frightened, lonely or unhappy is to go outside, somewhere they can be alone, alone with the sky, nature and God." Even though she could not go outside when she wrote this, she thought, "As long as this exists . . . this sunshine and this cloudless sky, and as long as I can enjoy it, how can I be sad?"

Often her mood was both happy and sad at the same time: "Every day I feel myself maturing, I feel liberation [of Holland from the Germans] drawing near, I feel the beauty of nature and the goodness of the people around me. Every day I think what a fascinating and amusing adventure this is! With all that, why should I despair?"

Anne's moods were influenced by more than being in hiding and hearing news of the war. She was a teenager, in between being a child and being an adult. This is an age when one's feelings often change from extreme happiness to desperate sadness.

Miep Gies wanted to encourage Anne to feel good about being grown up. She bought Anne a secondhand pair of high-heeled shoes. Miep wrote, "Never have I seen anyone so happy as Anne was that day. And quick, on went the shoes, and they fitted just right. She got very quiet then: she had never felt herself on high heels before. She wobbled slightly, but with determination, chewing on her upper lip, she walked across the room, and back, and then did it again. Just walking back and forth, up and back, more and more steadily each time."

News of the war did, of course, also influence Anne's moods. In the winter and spring of 1944, Holland was caught up in "invasion fever." The Dutch people were hoping the Allied forces from England and the United States would land in Europe and win back the countries that were under German control. Anne alternated between happiness and despair as the months passed and no Allied landing took place.

The Westertoren Church steeple as it looked from the top window of the annex

The invasion finally began on June 6, known as "D-Day." But the Allied forces would not liberate Amsterdam until ten months later. The people in the annex followed the troops' slow progress with pins stuck in a map on the wall.

THREE

Not All Bad Times

ANNE FRANK HAD a fun-loving nature, so not everything she did in the annex was serious. Soon after she moved in, she wrote a humorous "Guide to The Secret Annex," treating the hiding place as if it were a wonderful resort. The guide notes that the price is free, the diet is low fat, and "only the language of civilized people may be spoken, thus no German." The guide also advertises that there is a radio with broadcasts from London, New York, and Tel Aviv that one can listen to after 6:00 in the evening. "It is absolutely forbidden to listen to German news bulletins," she added.

Anne spent a lot of time looking at her collection of movie star photos, and she decorated her walls with these pictures. She also amused herself by imagining that her father had given her 150 guilders (quite a lot of Dutch money) and that she had gone to Switzerland to spend it.

The room in the
annex that Anne
shared with Fritz
Pfeffer—called
Mr. Dussel in
her diary

Anne had covered the
wall of her room with
pictures of celebrities
including the English
princesses Elizabeth
(who is now queen)
and Margaret, and
movie stars.

Dit is een foto, zoals ik me zou wensen, altijd zo te zijn. Dan had ik nog wel een kans om naar Holywood te komen. AnneFrank. 10 Oct. 1942

🔹 *"This is a photo as I would wish myself to look all the time. Then I would maybe have a chance to come to Hollywood." Anne Frank, 10 Oct. 1942.*

She made a long, detailed list of all the clothes and makeup she would buy. It included three bras in the "smallest size," an ice-skating outfit, and suntan lotion.

One evening, Anne and Peter Van Pels put on a show. She dressed up in one of his suits and he wore a dress of her mother's that was a "skin-tight" fit. She wrote, "The grown-ups split their sides laughing."

After they had been living together in the annex for almost two years, Anne and Peter began to feel romantically interested in each other. They spent a lot of time talking in Peter's room, looking out the window together, discussing the facts of life, and having a few brief kisses. Eventually, Anne realized that she needed a boyfriend who could express his feelings more openly than Peter. While she thought she was in love with him, though, she felt happier and more optimistic about the world and the future than she did at other times.

The people in the annex, often spurred on by Anne, tried to make special occasions as festive as possible. On Miep and Jan Gies's first wedding anniversary, July 18, 1942, the couple had dinner in the annex. Anne typed up a special menu for the occasion. It included "Bouillon a la Hunzestraat," named for the street where the couple lived, "roast beef Scholte," named for their butcher, and "Riz a la Trautmansdorf," which means rice as prepared in a cozy little village in Germany. Soon after that, Anne invited Miep and Jan to spend a night in the annex, a great treat for those in hiding. Miep and Jan saw first-hand how closed in their friends felt all the time.

Anne celebrated two birthdays in the annex. On June 12, 1943, when she turned fourteen, her father wrote a long poem for her. It included these lines:

The more difficult question, much harder to bear,
Is "What on earth do I have to wear?
I've got no more panties, my clothes are too tight,
my shirt is a loincloth, I'm really a sight!
To put on my shoes I must cut off my toes,
Oh dear, I'm plagued with so many woes!"

Anne wrote that her presents—a book on mythology and a lot of candy—made her "thoroughly spoiled." The next year, when she turned fifteen, Anne received underclothes, belts, a handkerchief, jars of yogurt and jam, books about art history and botany, a gold bracelet from Margot, and a "lovely bouquet of peonies" from Peter.

The families also celebrated St. Nicholas Day. St. Nicholas is the saint most connected with children. In many European countries, St. Nicholas Day, early in December, is more of an occasion for gift giving than Christmas, which is the more religious holiday. The Jewish families in the annex had never celebrated this holiday before, but Miep Gies thought they might enjoy it because it "is more a day for children than a day of religious observance." She also knew that the Franks were "liberal about religious practice."

The first year, Miep and Bep composed little rhymes for everyone, a St. Nicholas Day tradition. They also made small gifts. They put all the gifts and poems in a big basket covered with decorations and hid the basket.

Opekta-Works and the Secret Annex

1 Hermann, Auguste, and Peter Van Pels
2 Otto, Edith, and Margot Frank
3 Anne Frank and Fritz Pfeffer
4 Courtyard
5 Bookcase/secret entrance
6 Bathroom
7 Opekta-Works storeroom

Then Otto Frank led the other annex residents to the basket to surprise them.

The next year, Anne and her father composed rhymes for everyone for St. Nicholas Day. They put a poem in each person's shoe, then put all the shoes together in a big party basket.

The families also celebrated Chanukah, a Jewish holiday that takes place in early December. This holiday commemorates an ancient military victory by the Jews. It involves lighting candles for eight days and giving presents to children. On December 7, 1942, Anne wrote that the people in the annex celebrated Chanukah by exchanging a few small gifts, lighting candles for ten minutes, and singing a song.

FOUR

Living in Fear

THE SPECIAL OCCASIONS were the high points of life in hiding. There were also extremely difficult times. In such close quarters there were a lot of arguments. Anne felt that Mrs. Van Pels was always criticizing her, when all Anne was doing was displaying her naturally lively and outspoken personality.

There were arguments between the families about food. There often was not enough, and the food they did have soon became boring. Anne described their "food cycles," in which they had to use one type of vegetable over and over: "For a long time we ate nothing but endive. Endive with sand, endive without sand, endive with mashed potatoes, endive–and–mashed potato casserole. Then it was spinach, followed by kohlrabi, salsify [a plant with a root that tastes like oysters], cucumbers, tomatoes, sauerkraut, etc., etc." She also wrote that they ate pickled kale, which was a few years old and smelled so bad that

Food was scarce for everyone in Holland, not just for those in hiding. These children are eating tulip bulbs. Holland's tulips are usually valued for their blooms, but during the war they were prized for their food value. The bulbs are supposed to taste like sweet potatoes.

she used a handkerchief sprinkled with perfume to cover the smell.

Jews in hiding were not the only people suffering. Throughout Holland, the war brought shortages of everything people needed to live a comfortable life. The second winter in hiding, Anne would look out the window and see children without coats or hats begging for bread.

Around the time of her fourteenth birthday, Anne began squinting when she read and complaining of headaches. The people in the annex thought she probably needed glasses. Miep offered to take Anne to an eyeglasses store nearby for an examination. She said she would then go back alone to pick up the glasses, with some explanation for why she would be alone. That way Anne would only have to leave the annex once, and that trip would take less than an hour.

It was against the law for unregistered Jews to be out in the street, and Miep's idea frightened Anne. Miep suggested they go immediately so that Anne would not have time to become afraid. Everyone in the annex talked over the plan. Anne said she might faint with fear just at the thought of actually being in the street. But she said she would do it if her father wanted her to. The Franks told Miep they would give her an answer the next day. After talking it over again, they decided that it was too dangerous to go outside. "It's better if we all stay here together," said Otto Frank.

Behind this bookcase was the secret entrance to the annex. The staircase led up to the space where the Van Pels family slept, and behind the stairs were the rooms for Anne and her family. When burglars entered the building, everyone in the annex was afraid the burglars would hear them and find the entrance to their hiding place.

Dutch SS volunteers joined the Nazis in rooting out the Jews from the Netherlands

An attempted burglary at their building during
Easter weekend in 1944 gave Anne her biggest scare in
hiding. If the thieves had noticed that people were hiding
there, they could have alerted the police. The inhabitants
of the annex waited in terror for three days, barely daring

to breathe because they thought the police might come. Finally, their helpers came back to work and assured them that they had not been discovered.

The scare upset even Otto Frank, who was usually calm and optimistic. It also led to new rules that made life in hiding even more difficult than it had been. Peter was no longer allowed to open his window, for example, and no one could flush the toilet after 9:30 at night.

Anne had vowed to die bravely, like a soldier, if the break-in led the Nazi police to the annex. Once she felt safer, she realized she had a lot of courage and independence. She also knew she had a desire for justice. She vowed to make her voice heard, to "go out into the world and work for mankind."

FIVE

After the Diary

ANNE MADE HER last diary entry on August 1, 1944. On
that day she described herself as lighthearted and frolic-
some on the outside but said that her true, inner self was
deeper and more serious. She wished she could show this
quieter side to the others in the annex.

On the morning of August 4, 1944, a German policeman and four Dutch Nazi sympathizers burst into the
annex with their guns drawn. Otto Frank was about to
give Peter an English lesson upstairs. The policeman
emptied Otto Frank's briefcase and filled it with money
and jewelry. Anne's diary and other writings, which were
in the briefcase, fell to the floor. It was clear from the way
the intruders behaved that someone who knew a lot
about the annex had betrayed them, probably to get a re-
ward. No one has ever found out who it was.

The annex members went first to a German police

🕮 *Prisoners arriving at Auschwitz*

station, where they spent four days in a cell. On August 8, they were sent to Westerbork, a Nazi camp in northern Holland, near the German border. On September 3, they were put on a train with a thousand other people and sent to Auschwitz in Poland. Auschwitz was the largest of the six Nazi death camps, which were built specifically for the killing of Jews. Theirs was the last train to Auschwitz from Holland.

The two-day trip to Auschwitz was in train cars made for transporting cattle. It was suffocatingly hot, there were no bathrooms, and the people had nothing to eat or drink. The day after their arrival at the camp, more than half of the people were killed. They were sent into chambers that looked like big shower rooms. Instead of water, however, poison gas came out of the showerheads. The first group to be killed included children under fifteen. Because Anne had turned fifteen in June she was spared at this selection point.

Of those who remained, the men and the women were separated. Anne, Margot, their mother, and Auguste Van Pels walked together to Birkenau, a part of the camp built specifically for killing.

In Birkenau, the women had to stand for up to five hours at a time outside in the cold and wet weather while the Germans called out methodically to make sure everyone was there. Throughout the Holocaust, many thousands of people perished during these brutal roll calls. The women from the annex may have been assigned some work to do in the camp. They certainly were hungry and cold all the time.

The war was almost over. The Russians, who were fighting the Germans, were approaching the camps from

🎔 *Children behind barbed wire in Auschwitz*

the east. The Germans wanted to hide the evidence of their atrocities. They shot many prisoners and moved others to concentration camps farther west.

In October, Anne and Margot had to leave their mother and go to Bergen-Belsen, a concentration camp in Germany. Edith Frank-Holländer died on January 6, 1945, in Auschwitz. At Bergen-Belsen it was bitter cold and there was no food. The camp was severely over-crowded, so diseases spread among the prisoners.

Amazingly, Anne's old childhood friend, Hanne Goslar, was in another part of the camp at the same time. Someone from Amsterdam told her that the Frank girls were nearby. Anne and Hanne managed to speak across the barbed wire that separated them. Margot was too sick to leave her bed. Anne's first words to Hanne were that she "had no parents." She assumed her father had been killed.

Hanne described Anne as a "broken girl." Anne could not stand the lice in her clothes, so she had taken them off and was wandering around in icy cold weather wearing only a blanket. Another person who was with Anne and Margot said they were sleeping near the door in an unheated barracks, and every cold blast of air blew right on them.

Both girls got typhus, a disease spread by lice. Margot died in February or March 1945. Anne was totally alone and thought that everyone else in her family was dead. She died in March, just a few weeks before the Russians arrived at the camp and freed the prisoners.

Of the eight people who had lived in the annex, only Otto Frank survived the war. He was still at Auschwitz when the Russians liberated it. He went back to Amsterdam in June 1945 and moved in with Miep and Jan Gies. He knew his wife was dead but he hoped his daughters

The severe overcrowding at Bergen-Belsen contributed to the spread of disease. Anne and Margot Frank died of typhus in a barracks like this. This photo was taken by the British at the moment they liberated Bergen-Belsen.

were alive. In August he got the sad news that they, too, had died.

When it was certain that Anne had died, Miep gave the diary to Otto Frank. She had held onto it, hoping she would be able to return it to Anne. Otto Frank read it and was impressed by how accurately and vividly Anne had written about their life in hiding.

Mr. Frank showed Anne's diary to some friends, who urged him to publish it. He could not find a publisher, however, until a Dutch newspaper printed an article about the diary in April 1946. In the summer of 1947, an edition of 1,500 copies was printed in Dutch. It was soon translated into French, German, and English.

Anne Frank: The Diary of a Young Girl has now been translated into fifty-five languages, and more than twenty-five million copies have been sold. There are also plays and movies about Anne Frank. In 1995, *Anne Frank Remembered,* a movie by Jon Blair, won the

Miep Gies in 1988, receiving an award from the government of Israel. Miep worked with other Opekta employees to keep the residents of the annex supplied with food and books.

Otto Frank at the dedication of a school named in Anne's memory in Düsseldorf, Germany

To Betty Ann
from Mother
May 14, 1956

Anne Frank

THE DIARY OF A YOUNG GIRL

Anne Frank

TRANSLATED FROM THE DUTCH
BY B. M. MOOYAART-DOUBLEDAY
WITH AN INTRODUCTION
BY ELEANOR ROOSEVELT

Margot Frank

1952 GARDEN CITY, NEW YORK

DOUBLEDAY & COMPANY, INC.

*Title page of the first
American edition of
Anne Frank's diary*

Academy Award for best documentary. Miep Gies was in Hollywood with the director to accept the award.

In 1953, Otto Frank married a woman who had survived a concentration camp with her daughter. They lived in Switzerland until his death in 1980. He devoted his life to helping people comprehend the Holocaust through Anne's diary. The annex has been preserved as a museum

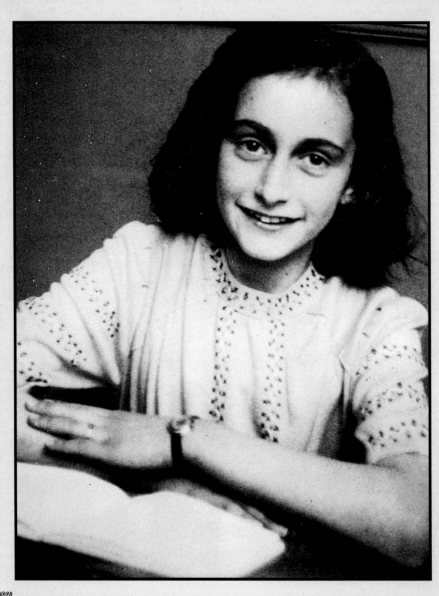

Photo of Anne Frank taken shortly before she went into hiding; there are no photos from the years in hiding.

in Amsterdam. It is called the Anne Frank House, and it is the most popular tourist attraction in Holland.

Anne Frank wanted to "go on living" after her death. She thought she would become a journalist, using what she recognized as her gift for writing to "work for mankind." Although Anne tragically did not live to enjoy it, she did become famous and is an inspiration to millions of people from all over the world. They have fallen in love with a girl who, while suffering through one of the darkest periods in history, found this to say: "Riches, prestige, everything can be lost. But the happiness in your own heart can only be dimmed; it will always be there, as long as you live, to make you happy again."

For More Information

Frank, Anne. *Anne Frank's Tales from the Secret Annex*. New York: Washington Square Press, 1982.

Frank, Anne. *The Diary of a Young Girl: The Definitive Edition*. New York: Doubleday, 1995.

Gies, Miep, with Alison Leslie Gold. *Anne Frank Remembered: The Story of the Woman Who Helped to Hide the Frank Family*. New York: Simon & Schuster, 1987.

Lindwer, Willy. *The Last Seven Months of Anne Frank*. New York: Anchor Books–Doubleday, 1991.

Schloss, Eva, with Evelyn Julia Kent. *Eva's Story*. New York: Berkley Books, 1990.

van der Rol, Ruud, and Rian Verhoeven. *Anne Frank: Beyond the Diary*. New York: Puffin Books, 1995.

OTHER BOOKS ABOUT THE HOLOCAUST

Auerbacher, Inge. *Beyond the Yellow Star to America*. Unionville, N.Y.: Royal Fireworks Press, 1995.

————. *I Am a Star: Child of the Holocaust.* New York: Prentice-Hall Books for Young Readers, Simon & Schuster, 1986.

Bachrach, Susan D. *Tell Them We Remember: The Story of the Holocaust.* Boston: Little, Brown, 1994.

Halliday, Laurel, ed. *Children in the Holocaust and World War II: Their Secret Diaries.* New York: Pocket Books, 1995.

Isaacson, Judith Magyar. *Seed of Sarah: Memoirs of a Survivor.* Urbana, Ill.: University of Illinois Press, 1990.

Siegel, Aranka. *Upon the Head of the Goat: A Childhood in Hungary 1939–1944.* New York: New American Library, 1981.

Toll, Nelly S. *Behind the Secret Window: A Memoir of a Hidden Childhood.* New York: Dial Books, 1993.

Volavkova, Hana, ed. *I Never Saw Another Butterfly: Children's Drawings and Poems from Terezin Concentration Camp 1942–1944.* New York: Schocken, 1993.

FOR ADVANCED READERS

Dawidowicz, Lucy S. *The War against the Jews: 1933–1945.* New York: Bantam Books, 1986.

Gilbert, Martin. *Atlas of the Holocaust.* New York: William Morrow and Company, 1993.

Johnson, Paul. *A History of the Jews.* New York: Harper & Row, 1987.

OTHER

The movie *Anne Frank Remembered* (Sony Pictures Classics, 1995) is the first ever eyewitness account of the life and legacy of Anne Frank. It was written, produced, and directed by Jon Blair.

The CD-ROM *Diary Maker* (Scholastic, Inc., the Anne Frank Center USA, and the Anne Frank House, 1996) features selections from the diary of Anne Frank and from the diaries of girls who have recorded their experiences during times of great hardship.

INTERNET SITES

Due to the changeable nature of the Internet, sites appear and disappear very quickly. Internet addresses must be entered with capital and lower-case letters exactly as they appear.

The Yahoo directory of the World Wide Web is an excellent place to find Internet sites on any topic. The directory is located at:
http://www.yahoo.com

Anne Frank Online:
http://www.annefrank.com/

The Anne Frank Education Trust UK is a nonprofit charity whose aim is to educate against all forms of racism and discrimination by explaining the history of Anne Frank and the Holocaust:
http://www.afet.org.uk/

Index

Page numbers in *italics* refer to illustrations.

About The Author

RACHEL EPSTEIN IS the author of *Bizspeak: A Dictionary of Business Terms, Slang and Jargon* (with Nina Liebman) and of four books on business and two on health for high school students. She wrote the shopping column for the *New York Observer* for five years and has written articles for the *Forward,* the *Wall Street Journal,* and the *Washington Post.* Ms. Epstein has been involved with volunteer work for Israel for twenty-five years. She is the mother of two grown children and lives in Brooklyn, New York, with her husband.